NA

DATE DUE

CASE CLOSED?!
40 MINI-MYSTERIES FOR YOU TO SOLVE

CASE CLOSED?!

40 Mini-Mysteries for You to Solve

JÜRG OBRIST

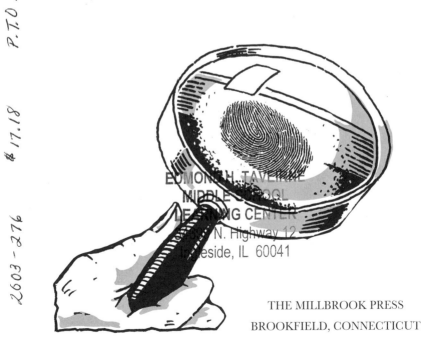

THE MILLBROOK PRESS
BROOKFIELD, CONNECTICUT

Published in the United States of America in 2003 by
The Millbrook Press, Inc.
2 Old New Milford Road, Brookfield, CT 06804

Originally published in Germany by dtv junior
www.dtvjunior.de

Library of Congress Cataloging-in-Publication Data
Obrist, Jürg.
Case closed?! : 40 mini-mysteries for you to solve / Jürg Obrist.—
[1st American ed.].
p. cm.
Summary: The reader can use visual clues and deductive reasoning
to help Daisy and Ridley solve forty puzzling mysteries.
ISBN 0-7613-2739-8 (lib. bdg.) ISBN 0-7613-1999-9 (pbk.)
[1. Detectives—Fiction. 2. Mystery and detective stories.]
I. Title.
PZ7.O14Cas 2003   [Fic]—dc21   2002154651

Library 5 4 3 2 1
Trade   5 4 3 2 1
Printed in the United States of America

CONTENTS

INTRODUCTION

DAISY PEPPER
& RIDLEY LONG,
PRIVATE DETECTIVES

Daisy and Ridley's office telephone won't stop ringing. The two detectives are busy around-the-clock. They're after shady crooks, sneaky thieves, and other swindlers. And they are very successful at solving even the trickiest mysteries!

You have the chance to be right where it happens. But watch out! There is a lot of swindling and fibbing going on. You must read the stories carefully, and observe the pictures very, very carefully in order to find the correct solutions.

You'd better get started. Ridley and Daisy are already on the job . . . and they will be grateful for your help!

MS. BLAZE AND
THE MYSTERIOUS GHOST

Ms. Blaze has called Daisy Pepper to come to her house immediately. Still shaking, Ms. Blaze stammers nervously as she explains what happened:

"Around 10:55 A.M. I went into the kitchen. Suddenly, someone covered with an odd white sheet appeared in the foyer. What looked like a ghost raced toward the entrance door. It was in such a hurry it banged into the door frame before it vanished into the hallway. Even though I was terribly shocked, I immediately realized that my prizewinning lottery ticket had vanished along with the ghost!"

Daisy is certain that this ghostly thief must be one of Ms. Blaze's neighbors. So she calls them together to ask each of them where they were at 10:55 A.M. Here are their answers:

Miss Dustley: "At that time I finished making the beds and then started cooking."

Mr. Radish: "I was grocery shopping, and have just now returned."

Mr. Ferguson: "I slept late and have just finished showering."

One of the three is lying, and must have played the ghost in order to steal Ms. Blaze's lottery ticket.

Which one is the thief?

A PRECIOUS SALT SHAKER COLLECTION

Doris Katz, from Northbies Inc., the famous auction house, is carrying a very valuable salt shaker collection. She is just arriving at the Central Train Station. At 10 A.M. her train will be leaving for Boston, where she will show the shakers to a potential buyer.

It just so happens that Ridley is bringing a friend to the train station at the same time. Also at the same time, Tony, a former salesman at Northbies, is secretly following Doris. He seems to be very well informed about this particular business trip of hers! He himself is a fanatical salt shaker collector and desperately wants to get his hands on her precious goods.

Doris puts down her suitcase for a moment to check the departure times. That's when Tony makes his move and then quickly disappears into the busy crowd.

But—bad luck! He didn't know that Ridley saw how he managed to snag Doris's costly collection. And, of course, Ridley's powers of observation tell him Tony's getaway path.

How are your powers of observation? Do you know how it happened and where Tony is headed?

THE LITTLE SILVER FLAT-TAIL BIRD

The gate to Milda Beak's birdcage is wide open. And the home of her beloved silver flat-tail birdie is empty! The little bird, an extraordinarily rare breed, has been stolen! Milda is certain about that!

She is also certain that Tim Wattsman, the handyman, had something to do with the birdnapping. Just the day before yesterday he told her that she could sell her unusual bird at the annual Bird Fair for a lot of money!

Ridley promises Milda to pay Wattsman a visit and check him out. But Wattsman only grumbles, "No way! I don't have Ms. Beak's bird. Actually, I can't stand birds."

Yet Ridley has very sharp eyes. Something in Wattsman's place proves that he is definitely hiding Milda's bird. He probably wants to sell it himself at the Bird Fair.

Do you have an eagle eye? What does Ridley discover?

ORLANDO,
THE DISGUISE ARTIST

Daisy is sitting in the bus on the way to the airport. She is sitting across from and one row behind Orlando, a very clever dealer of fake diamonds. She has instructions to keep an eye on him and prevent him from boarding a plane and fleeing the country. It's not hard for Daisy to spot the villain because he is wearing an enormous moustache!

But, when they arrive at the airport, Orlando suddenly disappears into the men's room. Daisy has no choice but to hide behind a column and wait for him to come out. But Orlando does not show up again at all!

She can only conclude that he must have disguised himself in the bathroom and come out as a different person. And he might already be on his way to the plane. Daisy is quite upset. How could she fall for such an obvious trick?! Did she really lose the lousy swindler?

But Daisy doesn't give up. She looks everywhere for the disguised diamond dealer. And finally, before it's too late, she spots him among the many travelers.

How does Daisy recognize him and where is he?

NOTHING BUT NOODLES!

The famous noodle factory, Mac–Aroni Inc. plans to renew its entire noodle program. Well-known noodle designers were invited to create a new, totally revolutionary "Noodle Collection 2003." Of course the matter is top secret!

But, as always, newspapers and TV stations are trying every possible way to get some inside information. They all want to be the first to break the news.

One day, Billy Ashly, the office clerk, observes through the milky glass of the boss's office door a very interesting incident. A man he's never seen in the office before is giving the secret noodle designs to a female newspaper reporter.

Billy is shocked. He decides to follow the woman. But he also wants to notify Ridley and Daisy, so they

can stop the intruder from getting the closely guarded noodle designs into the news. Billy is confused about what to do first. But in the meantime, the lady has already disappeared into the streets.

This is a job for you alone. Can you help him spot the woman?

CHOPPED DOWN IN SECRET

It's early in the morning. Jack Leavling is just returning from a fabulous party. But standing in front of his house, he is startled. He can't believe his eyes! The beautiful one-hundred-year-old oak tree in his backyard is lying on the ground. Cut down! "Who did this?" he gasps. At that moment it strikes him: Al Gripe, his neighbor who constantly complains about the oak blocking the sun on his porch!

Jack calls his old friend Ridley for help. And at 7:30 A.M. they ring Al Gripe's doorbell. As Al listens to their accusation, he becomes very angry. "I wasn't here last night. I visited my sister, Lizzy, and it was too late for me to return home. So I slept at her house and arrived here just five minutes ago. It's not possible to cut down your oak tree in such a short time!" he yells.

But Ridley notices a couple of things, which may cast some doubt on Al's story.

Do you notice them too?

THE TERRIFYING
KASIMODO GANG

Daisy and Ridley have heard rumors that the malicious Kasimodo Gang is in town. The two detectives have known the three Kasimodo brothers, Lucky, Teddy, and Nicky, for a long time.

Now there are fresh clues about another big job in the works. One of the brothers, Lucky, was seen in the Sharktooth Cafe drinking hot chocolate. Ridley and Daisy hurry to grab Lucky. But when they arrive, he is already gone. In his rush, though, he has left behind some evidence in the ashtray. "Look," Daisy laughs, "this tells us what the crooks are planning next!"

Where, and when, can Ridley and Daisy surprise the three brothers red-handed?

PERKEY HAS GOT BIG CHANGE

Perkey Dime steps into the office of Wells Largo Money Exchange. He smiles at the lady at the counter and shoves a fat bundle of bills through the opening of the glass window. "Please change these dollars into Swiss francs," he mumbles.

Just then someone softly taps his shoulder. It's Daisy Pepper, who kindly asks Perkey to follow her into the boss's office.

Why?

KITZO ON THE RUN

Kitzo appears to be a street magician. But actually his real magic trick is pulling money out of people's pockets. For weeks, Ridley tries to get a hold of Kitzo, yet the fake magician is always one step ahead of him. But yesterday Ridley got a tip that Kitzo might be hiding out with his former buddy, Brad Moody. Has the moment finally arrived for Ridley to snatch the hoodwinker?

Brad Moody, now retired from swindling, lives in a little house on the outskirts of town. As Ridley asks Brad about Kitzo, he just laughs, scratches his bald head and replies: "I live here all alone. Look around if you like. You can wave Kitzo's picture at me as long as you want. I haven't seen him for months!"

But Ridley knows better. He did look around! There is no question that Brad is lying and that Kitzo must be living with him.

How does Ridley come to this conclusion?

THE FIXED RACE

At the Johnstown Grand Prix the powerful racing cars are roaring through the racetrack. The famous car race is soon going into the all-decisive final laps. And once again, Michael Speedler has a clear lead.

Like all racing car drivers, Michael also needs to stop at the pits for refueling. His car is running on the special fuel F98, a mix specially developed just for his particular engine.

Michael, virtually undefeated at the track, recently grew suspicious of his fellow drivers. He fears some unscrupulous competitors will try anything to get him out of the race. That's why he has asked Daisy to keep an eye on his service crew.

And indeed, during refueling, Daisy spots some strange goings-on. A couple of phony crewmates are definitely planning to end Michael's winning streak!

What does Daisy see?

BELLA SPARK'S COSTUME PARTY

In the glamorous casino of Hiddlyville, Mayor Bella Spark throws a fancy costume party. The guests arrive in wonderful costumes, each one beautifully made-up and disguised.

In the middle of the banquet, Bella finds that an anonymous letter has been stuffed into her handbag. Attached is a photograph of a man. According to the letter there is a disguised criminal among the guests. It says he intends to set off the fireworks planned for midnight at an earlier, unexpected time so that in the confusion he can sneak away with the contest's grand prize.

Bella instantly calls Ridley for help. He mixes discreetly among the guests. Soon he smiles. It isn't hard to discover the strange intruder.
Do you agree?

29

THE SUMATRA SAPPHIRE

Warren Sparky appears to be very agitated. "My precious Sumatra sapphire, the most costly gem in my store, is gone!" he moans.

Daisy Pepper looks around his little store. "Please tell me what happened," she asks Sparky.

Warren Sparky begins: "It all went so quickly. Around 5:15 P.M. a man entered the store. He was interested in the Sumatra sapphire. We went into the customer's room so we wouldn't be disturbed. The customer carefully examined the valuable gem. Suddenly he shoved it into his pocket, jumped up, and ran out of the room. I couldn't follow him, because he kicked the door closed behind him. Then he fled into the street and disappeared into the evening crowd."

Daisy looks around and examines the display cases. Then she continues: "Is the valuable gem insured?" "Yes, it is," Sparky answers.

Daisy grins. It's clear to her that Sparky invented the whole story. Something in his statement cannot be right. It's obvious he is trying to stage an insurance fraud.

What's wrong with his story?

HOTEL FRAUD

"I had a sneaking suspicion, when the strange-looking guest signed in last night," sighs the owner of the Moosehead Hotel. "I couldn't read any of his scribbling at all!"

"Yesterday, when he arrived," she continues, "the scruffy man asked for the nicest room in the house. This morning he was gone—without paying his bill."

Ridley wants to see that particular room. "Maybe we'll find some clues," he says. Indeed, as he looks around, he can immediately tell where and when he could catch up with the cheating guest.

Can you tell too?

BIG TIME FOR A SUBSTITUTE

Three minutes to go! Panic in the Metro Theater of Hurlingfield. Bruno, the leading actor, who plays the Tin Man in *The Wizard of Oz,* is running around backstage. He's still in his bathrobe! By this time he is usually in his tin costume, ready to go onstage. But tonight he can't find it. "My costume is gone," he yells. "I can't find it anywhere!" So close to curtain time, it would be impossible to find a new one, especially in his size!

"We have no other choice. Leo, the understudy, will have to fill in," the director of the theater decides. And to Bruno's surprise, his replacement, skinny Leo, is standing at the stage door. He is ready and dressed in his own reserve tin costume.

Bruno is sure that something is fishy. He doesn't trust Leo at all. Fortunately, Daisy is in the audience, hoping to watch the show. She will come backstage to investigate.

Is there any evidence for Leo's involvement in Bruno's missing tin costume?

THE THEFT OF THE PINK MAGDALENA

Milford Ripple's most valuable stamp in his collection, the "Pink Magdalena," has disappeared—clearly it's been stolen!

Three people had visited today. One of them must have sneaked away with it while Milford was on the telephone in the living room.

Ridley Long listens carefully to their statements:

Billy, the plumber, fixed the leaking faucet in the bathroom. He claims that he didn't go into any of the other rooms.

Chuck Hostle, an insurance agent, lights a fresh cigar and replies, outraged: "I brought over some insurance papers, which I put on the table in the kitchen. Then I left right away!"

Trixie Dustly, the cleaning lady, swears that she was cleaning Milford's apartment, as she does every Thursday. But she would never set foot in Milford's study. He insists on cleaning it himself.

Ridley examines the study. Suddenly he smiles, because he finds a small piece of evidence that proves that one of the suspects is lying!

What is it, and who is the thief?

Billy

Trixie Dustly

Chuck Hostle

WHAT HAPPENED?

Ridley and Daisy are puzzled! They have received nine photographs taken by the surveillance cameras at the estate of Baroness Nadin. They show Stanley Ratz, known as a shady character, his monkey Lulu, the Baroness Nadin, and her boyfriend Roy Sleek. But the pictures have no numbers and are all mixed up together. In the right order they illustrate a very interesting occurrence at Nadin's fancy home! Especially since Ridley and Daisy desperately need some evidence in order to get a grip on Stanley and his monkey Lulu.

Can you put the pictures in the right order and tell what has happened?

THE INTERRUPTED CRUISE

Vacation, at last! Daisy yawns happily as she stretches herself on a deck chair on the cruise ship *Esmeralda*. They are quietly drifting through the waves, when all of a sudden the ship's bell rings an alarm.

"Stowaway on board!" the first officer yells. Sailors and cabin boys storm the deck and look for the intruder. One of the officers asks Daisy for assistance.

"There goes my peaceful holiday," she sighs, and begins her inquiries. But Daisy is relieved when she spots the lifeboat. It's clear that the person hiding there had to make a quick exit, because he or she left something behind. So it should be easy to find the stowaway on the boat. Daisy contentedly leans back and relaxes again.

Who can find the stowaway?

MARCO POLO IS GONE

Michele d'Angelo, the famous artist and sculptor, takes a stroll in the park behind his castle. Suddenly he stops. He is shocked! He stares in amazement at the front of the marble pedestal where his favorite sculpture of Marco Polo usually stands. The sculpture is gone. Just a hammer and some small stones lie scattered on the ground.

"What wicked scoundrel has stolen my Marco Polo?" Michele shouts. At once he calls Daisy, who happens to be a big fan of the artist.

Michele's porter leads Daisy to the scene of the crime. At the same moment, Mauro, the gardener, joins them, curious about the commotion.

Daisy inspects the site, asks questions, and finally turns to Michele: "This case is solved. The thief is right here among us!"

What brings Daisy to this conclusion and who is the thief?

THE MUSICAL DECORATIVE GARDEN DWARF

Hugo, the guard at the local Decorative Garden Dwarf Museum, runs through the halls. "Fidelio the fiddler has been stolen!" he yells. Fidelio is a sitting decorative garden dwarf that plays the violin. A rare and jolly figure indeed! Hugo immediately informs Dr. Leek, the director of the museum.

"I'll bet Misty Troller has something to do with this!" Dr. Leek snarls. "Get Ridley and Daisy. Only they can crack this case."

Ridley and Daisy decide to pay Misty a visit. She practically lives in her garden shed down at the river. Misty is obsessed with decorative garden dwarfs. She probably has the country's biggest private collection of these little figures. And she has tried to buy the missing Fidelio from the museum many times. But the director knows the dwarf's extraordinary value, so Misty never had a chance!

Ridley and Daisy take the narrow stairs down to Misty's dwarf kingdom. They are everywhere. Daisy can't count them all, there are so many. When they ask Misty about the theft of Fidelio, she is enraged. "I don't know anything about it," she claims. But Ridley and Daisy are not convinced by her strong denial.

Can they prove her wrong?

A SECRET VISITOR IN THE DRESSING ROOM

Lola Dearly, the well-known singer, is presently performing at Thunder Hall. But at the moment the artist is terribly upset. "Someone must have been in my dressing room while I was onstage," she claims. Her manager, Rob, wants Daisy to come and clear things up.

Daisy gets the story from Lola: "Even before I went onstage, while I was putting makeup on, I sensed that someone was secretly peeking into my dressing room. But because time was short I didn't take it seriously. However, now that I'm back from the show, I feel that someone must have physically been in here. Maybe even stole something!"

Daisy giggles: "You can call him a thief. But I think that he is just a great fan of yours."

Compare the two pictures and you will know what Daisy means!

THE SECRET MESSAGE

Waldo and Bruce have collected quite a lot of money with some phony checks. Right after their last crooked job, they split up to wait until things calmed down. Bruce hides with his grandmother, and Waldo brings their loot to a safe hiding place. He informs Bruce about it with a secret message. Then Waldo also goes into hiding for a while, as they have planned.

Shortly after, though, Bruce gets picked up by the police. They find Waldo's secret message on him. But they can't make heads or tails out of the strange signs.

"This is a job for Ridley and Daisy," one of the police officers says. "They're specialists in decoding stuff like this."

How's your decoding? If you're good at it, you'll know where they have to look next!

P.S. Later, Waldo also gets arrested. He too was hiding out at his grandmother's!

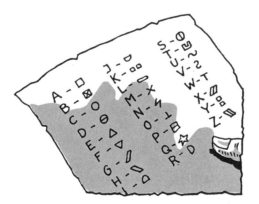

THE SHORT LIFE OF THE MARGERITHA KONOLLY

Rosie Green's greatest dream has come true! After many attempts, she has finally succeeded in breeding a Margeritha Konolly. She and her assistants Rita Pink and Aldo Stretch have worked hard to achieve this goal. It's the only plant of its kind. And tomorrow is the big day. Rosie plans to introduce the new species at the Plant Breeder Congress.

This plant is a "light-eater." It needs as much light as possible or it will die! That's why Rosie puts her creation right beneath the glass roof of the greenhouse.

But in the evening she discovers a most terrible thing! Her Margeritha Konolly has been moved into the darkness of the lowest shelf of the case. And now it's withered and lifeless! Rosie is certain that someone wants to prevent her appearance and success at the Plant Breeder Congress. A case for Ridley to solve!

Ridley examines the situation. He is sure that only Rita or Aldo could have had something to do with this. They're the only ones who have a key to the greenhouse. Here is what they say:

Aldo claims that he hasn't worked in the greenhouse for quite some time, because he was busy outside.

Rita explains that she has only been in the office the last three days, and has not set foot in the greenhouse.

But Ridley has sharp eyes, and can tell who is lying. Can you tell too?

A TRACE OF MICKEY COOL

For weeks, Ridley has been after the notorious safe-cracker, Mickey Cool. But he could never nab him.

One day after work, Ridley is on the way to the sub-way. Unexpectedly, Mickey pops up! Right in front of him. "This is it!" Ridley cheers. But at the same instant Mickey has disappeared again into the crowd. Ridley runs toward a person he thinks he recognizes, hoping that it's Mickey. He decides to follow him.

After trailing him for a while, Ridley arrives at a gloomy backyard of a blacksmith's shop. He guesses that the safecracker has disappeared into one of the buildings. Some of the lights are still on. When he peeks over the fence, his hunch is confirmed.

Do you know why?

GENERAL JEFFERSON IS MISSING

Baroness of Coleslaw is very upset. "General Jefferson has been stolen," she shouts out of the window of her mansion. Of course she means the famous painting of the general.

Can Daisy solve this theft? The Baroness has called her immediately. Everybody in the house is suspected as a potential thief. There is the maid, the cook, the chauffeur, the chimney cleaner, the gardener—and even the Baron and Baroness themselves!

Daisy carefully checks every corner of the estate. And soon enough she knows who the thief is.

Do you know too?

TUFFTEL'S NEWEST INVENTION

Albert Tufftel has just made the invention of his life. He created the formula to grow hair back. And it works! He has tried it on himself, and the results are astonishing. Tufftel can't wait to show his discovery to the world. The same evening he invites a couple of his colleagues to hear their opinions about his work.

But unfortunately, during the presentation the lights go out. A short circuit! There is total darkness in the lab. However, Tufftel is able to repair the problem. But when the lights go back on, he is shocked to discover that the formula for his tincture is gone! One of his colleagues must have quickly torn it off his writing pad in the darkness! No doubt, one of them wants to use Tufftel's invention for his own purpose. But luckily Tufftel also has invited Ridley this evening. And he has just arrived. He takes a quick glance at Tufftel's guests, and knows immediately who had "ripped off" Tufftel's promising new invention.

Who is the thief?

PHOTO PUZZLE

"Oh, no!" Daisy cries. By mistake she just tore up the wrong picture folder. She was tidying up their messy office. In front of her lie many scraps of photographs of three wanted scoundrels. She positively needs the one picture of Smokey Spitz, so she can recognize and follow him at the annual Coin Conference tomorrow. She got a tip that he will be attending.

She has no other choice but to try to put the puzzle together again! Luckily she has a police sketch of Smokey. All she actually needs to know is Smokey's identification number so she can reorder the picture from the lab.

What is Smokey's identification number?

THE LUCKY PIG'S BAD LUCK

At the Small Pets Beauty Contest in Nutsly Town the winner is being announced right this moment. And as predicted, Dolly Minsk's cute little pig Pinkey wins first prize! Dolly is overwhelmed and all the people want to shake her hand to congratulate her. As she turns around to embrace Pinkey, she discovers that her little pig is gone. Dolly looks everywhere. She calls its name, but Pinkey does not turn up.

Ridley, who is also at the contest with his dancing China mouse, offers Dolly his help. He is certain that Pinkey didn't just wander off, but clearly it must have been stolen!

Do you share his suspicion?

THE SEARCH FOR THE COFFEE CUP THIEF

Daisy pays Hussel Cuppler a visit for some questioning. He is first on her list of people suspected of stealing several china coffee cups at an antique auction last Saturday morning. But Hussel grins while smoking his cigarette: "I have no idea what you are talking about. Show me proof, if you have any. . . !"

Daisy left her bag on her motorbike outside. Quickly she rushes out to get it. When she returns, it's she who grins. Hussel is still sitting in the same spot as before, and it looks as if he hasn't moved an inch. But Daisy immediately notices what actually happened while she was gone. Hussel definitely has something to hide . . . and it's most likely the stolen coffee cups!

What happened while Daisy was outside?

A ROUND OF MIDNIGHT POKER

It's around midnight in the grungy Dungeon Bar when four guests get together for a game of poker.

Rozzi Flesh, a dubious playboy, Laurie Heart, the piano player, Bill Posh, the bartender, and Sam Moosley, a salesman, are playing in the back room of the bar. And as usual the stakes are substantial.

But in fact, the winner was clear even before the game began. The other three players are now losing a lot of money. If Ridley or Daisy were there, they could warn them in time!

Do you know who the sure winner is and why?

THE FAKE ENGRAVING

Art dealer Albie Forgefield appears to be very nervous. "You better show me proof that this engraving is a fake!" he shouts to Ridley and Daisy.

Albie was in the process of selling the engraving *Nibbling Girl* to the wealthy art collector Rocky Fuller. According to Albie, it's supposed to be the only available engraving left by Vincent Borinelli, the famous sixteenth-century artist. That's why it's so very valuable!

But Rocky Fuller got suspicious and asked for Ridley's and Daisy's opinion. Fuller thinks that the picture is a fake. And, of course, so do the two detectives.

Are they correct in their conclusion?

TRANSACTION IN THE SHOE STORE

"Agent 005 is in town!" Ridley whispers to Daisy. "Just the spy you've always wanted to catch red-handed! He is about to get some top-secret information from his colleague, Spy X. The plan is for the hidden transaction to take place inside the Happy Toes shoe store."

Shortly after, Daisy goes to the store and observes X entering. He then begins to try on many different shoes. Soon there are dozens of shoes scattered around. While the confused salesman is distracted, X hides a tiny microfilm in one shoe of a pair. He sneaks the other shoe under his coat. Finally, he buys a pair of slippers and leaves the store. Before the salesman is able to clean up, 005 arrives. He wishes to try on some sandals. All he has to do is find the single shoe with the hidden film among all the others. Daisy is waiting for just that moment.

In which shoe is the secret film?

THE BIG MR. UNKNOWN

Dirk Crookly is a strange figure. He is involved in some dubious dealings. Ridley has known of him for years, but has not been able to find proof of any wrongdoing. Ridley is also aware that Dirk is working for Mr. Unknown, the head of a shady organization. And Ridley would very much like to know more about this Unknown fellow too.

Today Ridley spots Dirk with a package under his arm on the way to the post office. He is mailing it to his boss! But Ridley can't make out the complete name and address.

As soon as the post office closes in the evening Ridley checks all the packages brought in during the day. For Ridley, it will be easy to get the name and address of big Mr. Unknown.

How about you? Can you make the Unknown name and address known?

SWEET TOOTH

Baker Frank Sweetler and his bakery are famous for his delicious "Sweetler's Dreampatties." People even line up in front of the store to buy some of the sweet treasures.

This morning, just before Sweetler opens his store, he makes a dreadful discovery! All the Dreampatties he had made for today are gone. Five minutes ago they were in the special refrigerated case in the baking room. Now it's empty. "One of my employees must have taken them while I was on the phone just before," he grumbles. And that would be Pelle, the bookkeeper, Wilma, the saleslady, or Donald, the delivery boy.

Daisy, who luckily was waiting among a lot of other customers for the opening of the store, can help. She knows immediately who the thief with the sweet tooth is.

Do you know too?

MR. SCHUMMEL TRIES HARD

Ridley Long has just arrived at Zurich Airport in Switzerland. He is standing in the passport control line, waiting to enter the country. He wants to visit his great-aunt, who lives here.

Rollbert Schummel, the man in front of him, is showing his passport to the Immigration Officer. He too just arrived, on the same plane as Ridley.

The officer scratches his forehead. "Well, Mr. Schummel, you can't fool me," he says. "Your passport is a real fake, isn't it!" Schummel protests wildly. However, the officer is very sure of himself. Ridley, who introduces himself as a detective, takes a quick look at Schummel's passport. He can only agree that it is, indeed, a fake.

Why are they so sure about this?

FROM LOCKED-UP TO THE BASEBALL GAME

The twins Stan and Laurel look identical. Nobody could ever tell who is who! Both were serving time in Timblewood Prison. Were! Now they are happily on the loose. The trick with the hidden file in a loaf of bread has worked once again. The guard discovered the sawed-through iron rods shortly after they had fled Timblewood!

Ridley, though, is already on their tail. Their trail leads to the northern part of the city, right to the baseball stadium. Luckily for Stan and Laurel, thousands of spectators are just pouring into the stadium. The game will begin in half an hour. Stan and Laurel mix in with the crowd. And—good thinking!—they each take a seat in the stands, but not next to each other.

Ridley has a hard time spotting them in the rowdy group. But fortunately he has very good eyes.

Do you too?

DIRTY FINGERS

Arthur Pinslow, the goldsmith, is furious. Last night the spectacular necklace of Hollywood star Betty Goose was stolen. He had replaced some gold pieces on it.

Daisy, specialist in jewelry cases, inspects Pinslow's store very carefully. She is everywhere with her magnifying glass. "Here we are," she says triumphantly. "There is a nice big fingerprint right on the showcase. This should do it. All I have to do is to compare it with our files in the office."

It doesn't take her long when she checks with her catalog. Daisy now knows who to look for.

What is the name of the person who matches the fingerprint?

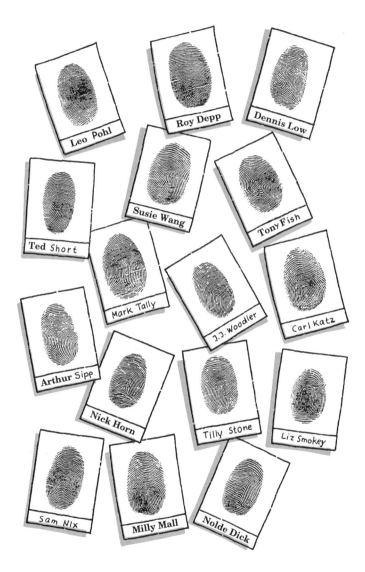

BEAUTY CONTEST WINNER

Sandy Glooming has recently won the Beauty Contest of Plow City. Since then she hears strange sounds at night in the staircase in the hall. She tells Ridley that she thinks she knows who is sneaking around there in the dark! "It could be Mary Jellous. She lost against me in the contest. And I know that she desperately wants to find out the brand of my diet mix," Sandy says.

Ridley inspects Sandy's place and then visits Mary. Scornfully, she says, "I have never been at her house. I don't even know where she lives!" But despite her reaction, Ridley agrees that Sandy is on the right track with her suspicion.

How does he know?

THE PIRANHA MOTH

Professor Wingfly, owner of a world-famous collection of living butterflies, is expecting an important shipment from Australia. When the package containing twelve extremely rare butterflies finally arrives at his house, the Professor is very surprised. When he opens the container, instead of twelve butterflies he counts thirteen of them. And, as an expert, he can immediately spot that one of the beautiful butterflies is actually a Piranha moth. This dangerous species can eat up all the other butterflies within a very short time. Somebody who must be very jealous of Professor Wingfly and his success has smuggled the destructive moth into the container. Of course the saboteur is hoping that the hungry little beast will do its job and harm Wingfly's butterfly collection.

Ridley and Daisy have just arrived. They need proof to confirm the Professor's claim that someone wants to wreck his life's work. Wingfly hands the two detectives the delivery papers, where all the butterflies he ordered are shown.

Who can find the dangerous Piranha moth?

THE ANONYMOUS THREAT

Count Dogstailer finds an anonymous note on the little marble table in his study. Some wicked person is trying to get the Count's valuable gold ring. It's an heirloom of his great-grandfather and is very dear to him.

Daisy looks at the note. Count Dogstailer assures her that nobody other than his servants has access to his study. Daisy therefore concludes that either the butler, the gardener, or the cook could have written the threatening note. Daisy paid each one of them a visit where they work. Soon it's clear to her who is wild about the Count's gold ring.

Who is the anonymous note writer?

PIGSBONE'S DELICIOUS HAM

It's Friday evening, 6:00 P.M. Ridley is about to leave the office. He is looking forward to a nice quiet dinner with his friend, Hal. In the hallway he hears the voices of Mrs. Sourtoe and her neighbor, Hank Loomy. Both are involved in a loud discussion with the delivery boy from Kostling's Deli.

Mrs. Sourtoe ordered a Pigsbone's ham from Kostling this morning. In the late afternoon the ham still hadn't been delivered. So Mrs. Sourtoe called and complained about the delay.

Kostling's delivery boy immediately came over to assure Mrs. Sourtoe that he actually had delivered that Pigsbone's ham this morning. "The problem is that you weren't in," he explains to her. "So I rang the doorbell at Mr. Loomy's. He agreed to hold the ham until your return!" But Hank Loomy wildly shakes his head from side to side and shouts, "Just a second, this is not true. I have never seen the delivery boy or that ham you are talking about. In fact, I was at the Castlebrew Horse Races the whole day!"

Mrs. Sourtoe is very confused. "One of you two is not telling the truth and probably wants to have that ham for yourself for dinner."

Luckily, Ridley has overheard everything. He joins them and tells Mrs. Sourtoe who is keeping that juicy Pigsbone's ham for himself.

How does Ridley know who kept the ham?

ANSWERS

Ms. Blaze and the Mysterious Ghost   Page 8
Mr. Ferguson was the ghost and therefore he is also the thief.
If he had just finished showering, his hair would still be wet.
He also wouldn't wear a shirt and a tie underneath his
bathrobe. The bandage on his forehead must be from the
bang into the door frame.

A Precious Salt Shaker Collection   Page 10
Tony has exchanged suitcases. Since he used to work in the
same agency, he has exactly the same suitcase as Doris. You
can find him running with hers at the top of the stairs toward
the restaurant.

The Little Silver Flat-Tail Bird   Page 12
Since Tim Wattsmann can't stand birds, why would he have
birdseed on the shelf under his kitchen counter? He must
have stolen Milda's silver flat-tail birdie so he could sell it at
the annual Bird Fair himself!

Orlando, the Disguise Artist   Page 14
Orlando has dressed himself in a traditional Arab's robe. He
is at the corner of the newsstand at the left. We know it's him
because he is still carrying the same package as on the bus.

Nothing But Noodles! Page 16

The sneaky female reporter is about to cross the street, just to the right of the tree that is being trimmed. The hairdo and the short-sleeved shirt are a dead giveaway, and she is carrying the case with the noodle designs under her arm.

Chopped Down in Secret Page 18

Al Gripe is lying. He wasn't gone the whole night. If Al had really come home five minutes ago he would have brought in the morning paper and the milk. Also, his breakfast has been made and is sitting on the table.

The Terrifying Kasimodo Gang Page 21

The torn-up note in the ashtray gives away where the gang plans to pull their next job. Ridley and Daisy just have to go there. The note says:

> Lucky, Get ready Next Saturday at midnight at the Peoples Penny Bank! Nicky

Perkey Has Got Big Change Page 23

The bills Perkey wants to change are clearly counterfeit. There are 5's in three of the corners, but a 3 in the upper-left-hand corner.

Kitzo on the Run Page 24

On the bureau to the right lies a comb with some hair in it. Brad is bald—therefore someone else has to live with him. It must be Kitzo, who, by the way, has plenty of hair!

The Fixed Race Page 27

The phony crew members are just about to fill Michael's fuel tank with water instead of F98.

Bella Spark's Costume Party Page 28

The lottery fan is dressed up as a sailor. He stands between the lady with the sun hat and the knight. He is recognizable from the ring in his left ear.

The Sumatra Sapphire   Page 30

Mr. Sparkey says that the thief kicked the door to the customer's room closed behind him. This is impossible since the door opens to the inside of the customer's room. Sparkey clearly wants to collect some money from the insurance company.

Hotel Fraud   Page 32

According to the torn-off ad from the newspaper the cheating hotel guest will be at the movies tonight. He and Camilla will see *On the Run* at 8 P.M.

Big Time for a Substitute   Page 34

Bruno is right! Leo has taken Bruno's tin costume and hidden it in his own dressing room. He desperately wants to play the Tin Man at least once in his career.

The Theft of the Pink Magdalena   Page 36

Ridley finds a stump of a cigar under the armchair in Milford's study. It's the exact same brand that Chuck Hostle smokes. He has sneaked into Milford's study and taken the Pink Magdalena.

What Happened?   Page 38

The right order of the pictures is:

D,I,B,H,G,E,F,C,A.

This is what happened:

D) Stanley and monkey Lulu watch Roy Sleek driving up to see his girlfriend Baroness Nadin. I) She is greeting him at the door. B) In the house Roy presents Nadin with a precious necklace. H) Nadin is very happy. G) They both step out of the room, leaving the necklace on the dresser. E) Stanley sends Lulu up to the open window. F) The monkey gets the valuable necklace. C) Lulu brings it back to Stanley. A) Roy and Nadin return and are shocked to see that the necklace had been stolen.

The Interrupted Cruise   Page 41
The stowaway forgot his shoe when he had to flee the lifeboat. He can be found on the top deck, on the left, next to the officer with the binoculars.

Marco Polo Is Gone   Page 42
Among the scattered stones on the ground you can see a tiny button. It belongs to the uniformed jacket of Michele's porter. Consequently, he must have stolen Marco Polo.

The Musical Decorative Garden Dwarf   Page 45
Ridley and Daisy can spot Fidelio in Misty's garden shed. She hid the dwarf in a box right next to the entrance.

A Secret Visitor in the Dressing Room   Page 46
The peeker through the keyhole is also the intruder. He has taken Lola's picture, which was hanging at the upper-right-hand corner of the mirror. He must be a big fan of hers indeed.

The Secret Message   Page 49
The message is:

BRUCE
BAG WITH MONEY IS AT CASTLE CROWBEAK
BEHIND CHIMNEY
WALDO

The hidden moneybag is behind the second chimney from the left.

The Short Life of the Margeritha Konolly   Page 50
Rita Pink has a lot of cactus prickles on her coat. They surely can't be from the office! They must be from the greenhouse! When Rita took down the Margeritha Konolly to put it into the shade on the lower shelf, she bent over the cactus. The prickles give her away.

A Trace of Mickey Cool   Page 52
Ridley discovers Mickey's monogrammed toolbox in the Old Blacksmith's shop. It's the same toolbox Mickey carried when he came out of the subway.

General Jefferson Is Missing   Page 54
The missing painting is already packed into the trunk of the car. The chauffeur has stolen the picture in order to sell it to a rich art lover.

Tufftel's Newest Invention   Page 56
Ridley immediately sees that the woman standing on the right is the thief. She is carrying the torn-off formula with other papers under her arm.

Photo Puzzle   Page 59
The identification number of Smokey Spitz is: 479901

The Lucky Pig's Bad Luck   Page 60
Ridley's suspicion is correct. The thief has put Pinkey into his shoulder bag and run off. You can spot him in the same row as Dolly's booth at the right edge of the picture.

The Search for the Coffee Cup Thief   Page 62
While Daisy was outside, Hussel took the black bag from the shelf on the left. When Daisy returns she notices a key missing from the board on the wall. The key is now in the cabinet's lock. So Hussel must have hidden the bag—most likely with the coffee cups—in there.

A Round of Midnight Poker   Page 64
The sure winner in this game is Sam Moosley. (His initials are on his briefcase behind him.) The crooked cheater still has two aces in his hand. On the table, however, are already three aces. Only four of each kind are in a deck of cards.

The Fake Engraving   Page 67
It couldn't be a worse fake! There definitely weren't telephones in the sixteenth century!

Transaction in the Shoe Store Page 68

The single shoe with the hidden microfilm is to the left of the salesman's head, right above his ear.

The Big Mr. Unknown Page 70

The package we are looking for is on the shelf to the left of the office sign. The name and address of Mr. Unknown is:

Mister Englebert No
5 Moonway
Boston

Sweet Tooth Page 72

There are footprints of sneakers in the flour on the floor. Only Donald, the delivery boy, is wearing sneakers, so he must be the thief with the sweet tooth.

Mr. Schummel Tries Hard Page 75

Nobody can be born on February 30. This month has only 28 days and every 4 years 29 days!

From Locked-Up to the Baseball Game Page 76

Stan is sitting in the first row, right behind the ice cream vendor, slightly to the left. Laurel took a seat in the upper-left part of the stands. He is behind the man with a black beard, slightly to the right. Or is it the other way around?

Dirty Fingers Page 78

Daisy has to look for J.J. Woodler!

Beauty Contest Winner Page 80

Ridley has discovered a lady's glove on Sandy's staircase. He finds the matching glove of the pair in Mary's apartment. It's on the lowest shelf under the TV set. Mary obviously must have been at Sandy's house.

The Piranha Moth Page 83

You can find the dangerous Piranha Moth in the upper-right corner of the picture.

The Anonymous Threat   Page 84

Daisy notices the misspelling of "Tusday" on the note. She spots the same mistake on the cook's menu plans for the Count. So it's the cook who wrote the threatening note to get her hands on his gold ring.

Pigsbone's Delicious Ham   Page 87

Hank Loomy is the one who is lying. He claims that he was at the Castlebrew Horse Races the whole day. According to the poster on the street, the horse races are on Saturday the 19th. Today, however, is Friday the 18th. Too bad that he won't be able to enjoy that juicy ham for dinner!

ABOUT THE AUTHOR/ ARTIST

Jürg Obrist studied photography at the Arts and Crafts School in Zurich, Switzerland. He then moved to the United States, where he lived for many years. At the moment he is back in Zurich with his family, doing freelance illustration and writing articles for teen magazines.

The author originally wrote this book in German, but his years in the United States perfected his English to the point that he was also able to be the translator for this edition. The job was a particular challenge because the words in the artwork had to be translated—but no problem. Jürg is also the illustrator of the original edition, so he was able to redo the calligraphy as well.

This is the first in a series of three mini-mystery books, all of which have been very popular with young would-be detectives in Germany as well as in France and South Korea.